disc

My Path to Math

1 2 3 4 5 6 7 8 9

Area

Marsha Arvoy and
Dorianne Nardi

Crabtree Publishing Company
www.crabtreebooks.com

Author: Marsha Arvoy and Dorianne Nardi
Publishing plan research and development:
    Sean Charlebois, Reagan Miller
    Crabtree Publishing CompanyCoordinating
Editor: Reagan Miller
Proofreader: Crystal Sikkens
Editorial director: Kathy Middleton
Project coordinator: Margaret Salter
Coordinating editor: Chester Fisher
Series editor: Jessica Cohn
Project manager: Kumar Kunal (Q2AMEDIA)
Art direction: Cheena Yadav (Q2AMEDIA)
Cover design: Jasmeen Kaur (Q2AMEDIA)
Design: Kanika Kohli (Q2AMEDIA)
Photo research: Anubhav Singhal and Noor Zaidi (Q2AMEDIA)

Photographs:
Istockphoto: Sze Kit Poon: p. 3, 4, 6, 8, 10, 12, 13, 14, 16, 18, 20, 22, 24;
    yasinguneysu: p.13; Cliff Parnell: p. 21 (bottom)
Q2AMedia Art Bank : 5, 7, 8, 9, 10, 11, 13, 15, 17, 18, 19, 23.
Other images by Shutterstock

Library and Archives Canada Cataloguing in Publication

Arvoy, Marsha.
    Area / Marsha Arvoy and Dorianne Nardi.
        p. cm. -- (My path to math)
    Includes index.
    ISBN 978-0-7787-6780-0 (reinforced lib. bdg. : alk. paper) -- ISBN 978-0-7787-6789-3 (pbk. : alk. paper)
    1. Area measurement--Juvenile literature. I. Nardi, Dorianne. II. Title. III. Series.

QC104.5.A78 2011
516--dc22

2010004496

Library of Congress Cataloging-in-Publication Data

Arvoy, Marsha.
    Area / Marsha Arvoy and Dorianne Nardi.
        p. cm. -- (My path to math)
    Includes index.
    ISBN 978-0-7787-6780-0 (reinforced lib. bdg. : alk. paper) -- ISBN 978-0-7787-6789-3 (pbk. : alk. paper)
    1. Area measurement--Juvenile literature. I. Nardi, Dorianne. II. Title. III. Series.

QC104.5.A78 2011
516--dc22

2010004496

Crabtree Publishing Company

www.crabtreebooks.com   1-800-387-7650

Printed in China/082010/AP20100512

Published in Canada
Crabtree Publishing
616 Welland Ave.
St. Catharines, ON
L2M 5V6

Published in the United States
Crabtree Publishing
PMB 59051
350 Fifth Avenue, 59th Floor
New York, New York 10118

Published in the United Kingdom
Crabtree Publishing
Maritime House
Basin Road North, Hove
BN41 1WR

Published in Australia
Crabtree Publishing
386 Mt. Alexander Rd.
Ascot Vale (Melbourne)
VIC 3032

Contents

Learn About Area

Mrs. Jackson's math class is learning about **area**. Area tells how much **surface** there is.

We measure surfaces using **square units**. Square units come in different sizes.

Square centimeters and **square inches** are small. They can measure smaller things, such as the surface of a book. **Square meters** and **square miles** are large. They measure larger areas, such playgrounds.

Activity Box

Why would a teacher want to know the area of a classroom rug?

The teacher shows the class an area that is covered by 144 square units.

square unit

Measure Area

Mrs. Jackson shows how to measure the top of a book. She uses square tiles. She places the tiles close together on the book. Then she counts the tiles. The area is 8 square units.

The tiles cover the top of the book. They fit well. However, square units do not always fit a surface perfectly. This is why we measure area to the **nearest whole unit**. Don't count a tile if less than half of it covers the surface. Count a tile if half or more can fit.

Activity Box

Lay a book on a table. Find the area of its front cover. Use square tiles of the same size. Measure to the nearest whole unit.

Fit as many tiles as possible. The fit does not have to be perfect, but it has to be close!

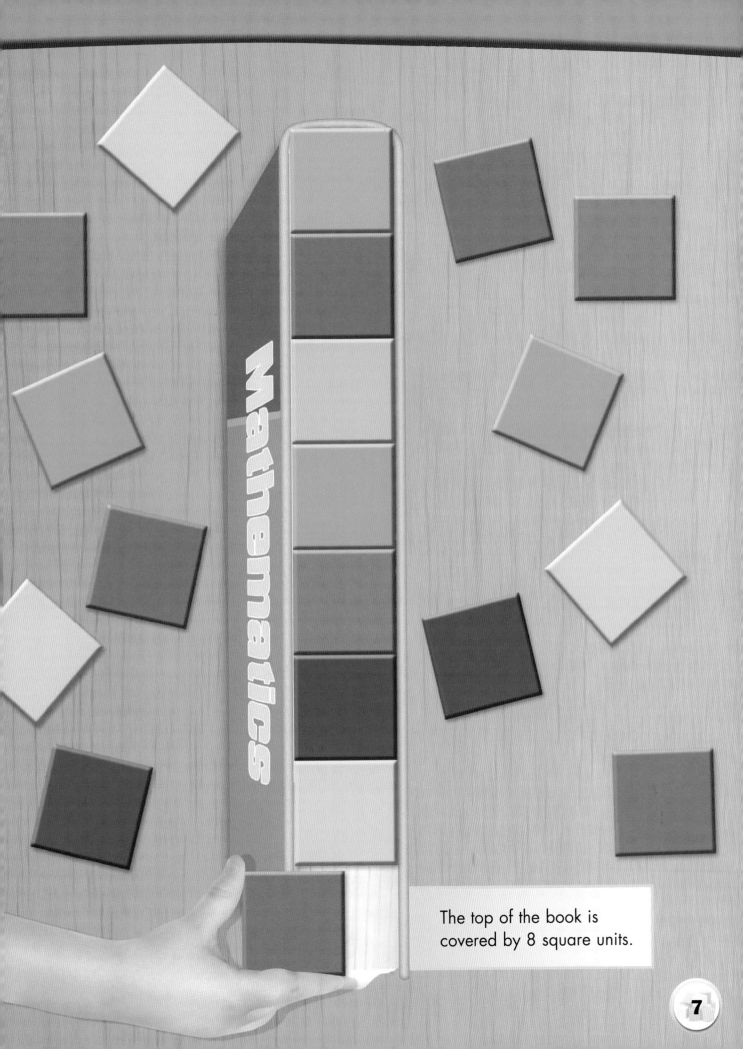

The top of the book is covered by 8 square units.

Standard Units

Sarah and Jeffrey are partners. They want to measure the area of a journal using pattern blocks. They cover the surface of their journal with blocks.

journal

The children use 11 pattern blocks to cover the journal. Then they notice that the blocks are different sizes. This means that the blocks are **nonstandard units**.

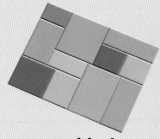

pattern blocks

Mrs. Jackson explains that they need to use square units to measure area. Square units are **standard units**. All the squares should be the same size.

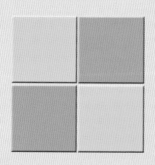

square tiles

Activity Box

Find a cereal box. Find its area using square units. Use square units that are all the same size. Use a standard size when you measure.

Use a standard unit to measure area. Pattern blocks are not standard.

incorrect attempt

correct attempt

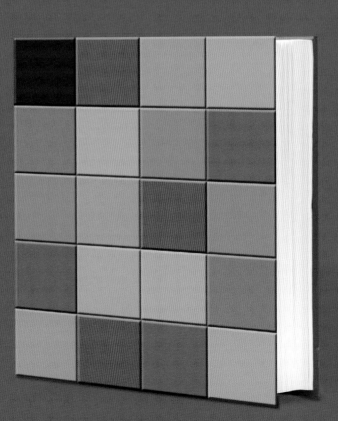

Units for Paper

Mrs. Jackson shows the class a piece of paper. She explains that there are two standard units that can be used to measure the area of the paper. In some parts of the world, a one-inch square is used. It measures area in square inches. In other parts of the world, a one-centimeter square is used. It measures area in square centimeters.

It is important to record the standard unit being used. Jeffrey asks, "Why?" She tells him to practice finding area to find out why.

Activity Box

Trace the square centimeter and square inch below. Cut them out. Then measure the area of a piece of paper in square inches and square centimeters.

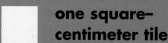 **one square–centimeter tile**

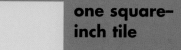 **one square–inch tile**

Jeffrey measures a piece of paper using square inches.
He writes his answer: _____ **square inches**.

The same sheet of paper can be measured using different square units.

He measures the same paper using square centimeters.
He writes his answer: _____ **square centimeters**.

Square Measures

Jeffrey measures the area of a block using square centimeter tiles. He finds that the area is 12 square centimeters. He records his **measurement** using square centimeters.

Next, he measures the same block using square inch tiles. He finds that the area is about 2 square inches. He records this measurement using square inches.

Jeffrey **compares** what he recorded. He discovers that the numbers are very different. He realizes that it is important to record the standard unit of measurement that is used.

Activity Box

Choose a small object and measure its area. Try using square–centimeter tiles. Then try using square–inch tiles. Compare your answers.

Jeffrey measures the area of his blocks.

Grid Paper

Mrs. Jackson shows the class a math tool called **grid paper**. Grid paper has boxes on it. Each box is the same size.

We are able to measure area using grid paper. We can use grid paper that shows square centimeters. We can also use grid paper that shows square inches.

Sarah draws a picture of a house on centimeter grid paper. She counts how many squares she colored in to make the house. She records the area using square centimeters.

Activity Box

Draw a picture of your house on grid paper. Count the boxes to find the area.

What is the area of the door? Count the number of boxes in the door.

Estimating Area

Sarah and Jeffrey trace their feet onto one-inch grid paper. First, they count the boxes that cover Sarah's foot. They find that the area of her foot is 24 square inches.

Then they **estimate** the area of Jeffey's foot. An estimate is a guess people make using things that they know. His foot looks a bit bigger than Sarah's foot. They estimate that his foot is 25 square inches.

Next, they count the boxes. They were close! The area of his foot is 26 square inches.

Activity Box

Trace your foot onto grid paper. Estimate the area first. Then count the boxes to find the area.

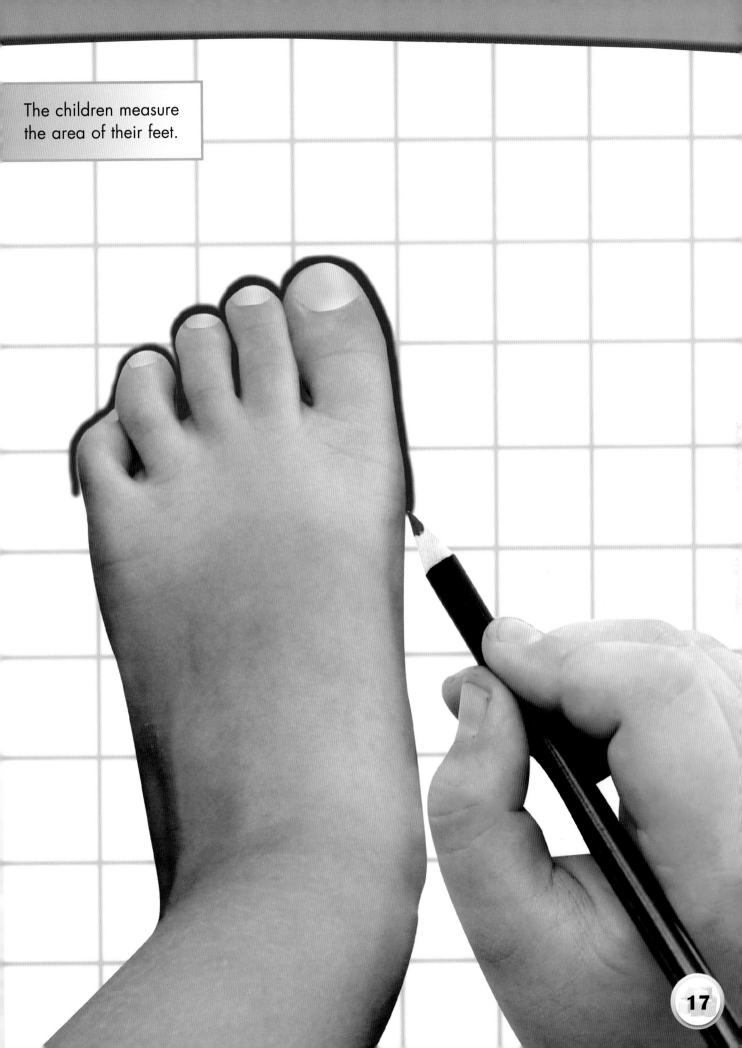

The children measure the area of their feet.

Geoboards

A **geoboard** is a square board with pegs. The pegs form squares. Each square is the same size. Rubber bands can be placed around the pegs. The rubber bands form shapes on the board.

Mrs. Jackson shows Sarah and Jeffrey how to make a square on their geoboard. She tells them to find the area of the square by counting the boxes inside the rubber band.

Then Sarah and Jeffrey try making **rectangles** on their geoboards. They find the area of the rectangles by counting the boxes.

area

Activity Box

Look at the square on the geoboard. Can you find the area by counting the boxes inside the square?

If you have a geoboard, use a rubber band to make a square. What is the area of your square? How many of those squares would be needed to cover the geoboard?

The children make rectangles on their geoboards, too.

Measure to Fit

Sarah and Jeffrey have learned about area. They have learned about the tools used to measure area. Mrs. Jackson tells them that she wants them to use what they have learned.

She says that she is getting a new computer for the classroom. The area of the computer is 70 square inches. She wants to know if the computer will fit on the small table near her desk.

Sarah and Jeffrey use one-inch square tiles to measure the table. They find that the area is 75 square inches. The computer will fit!

Activity Box

Why is it important to know about area? What kinds of things are built using area?

How many square units are
shown in the rectangle?

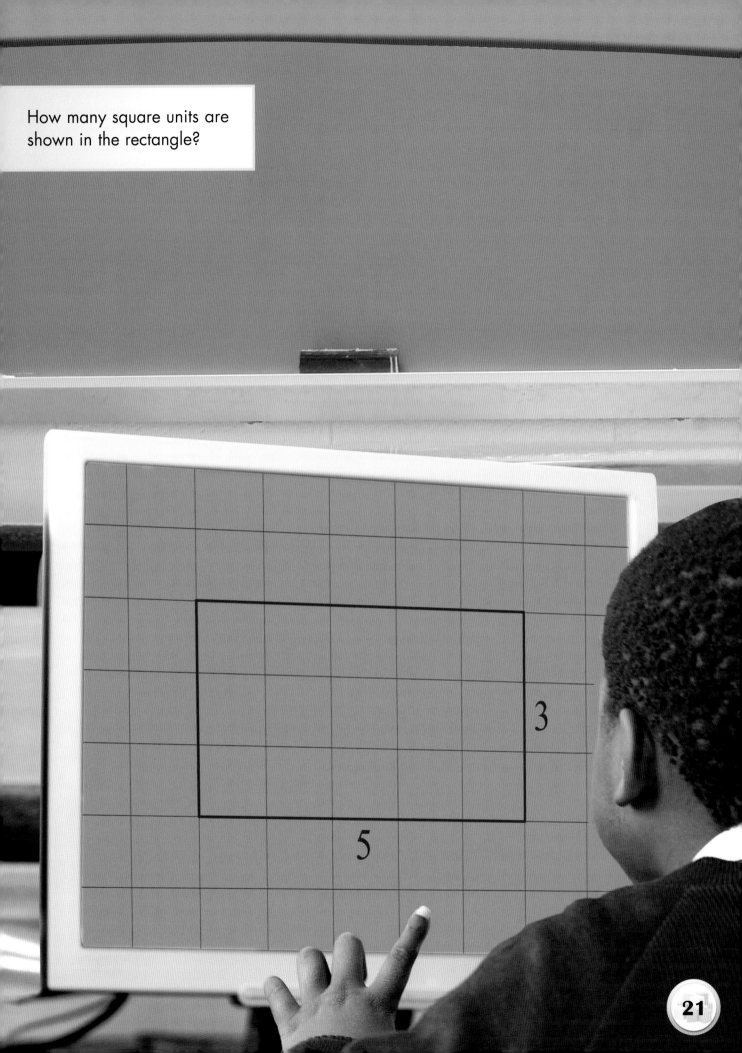

3

5

Glossary

area A measure of a surface

compares Shows how things are alike and different

estimate To use what you know to guess an answer, or the guess itself

geoboard A board that has pegs arranged in an evenly spaced grid

grid paper Paper ruled into small squares of equal size

measurement The size of an object

nearest whole unit The number of units found by rounding up or down

nonstandard units Objects that are not square units but are used to measure

rectangles Shapes with four straight sides and four right angles; not all sides are the same size but opposite sides are the same

square A shape that has four straight sides of the same length and four right angles

square centimeters Units of area in which all sides equal one centimeter

square inches Units of area in which all sides equal one inch

square meters Units of measure in which all sides equal one meter

square miles Units of measure in which all sides equal one mile

square units Units of measure with four equal sides

standard units Objects used to measure that are square units

surface The top part of an object

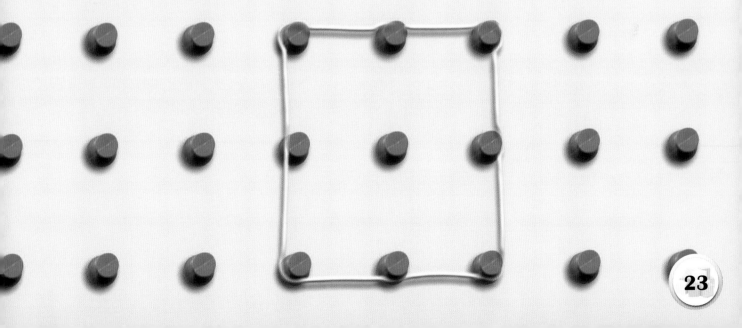

Index